MW00618426

Sanjeev Kapoor

Fun Food for Fussy Kids

In association with Alyona Kapoor

PopulaR prakashan

www.popularprakashan.com

Published by
POPULAR PRAKASHAN PVT. LTD.
301, Mahalaxmi Chambers
22, Bhulabhai Desai Road
Mumbai - 400 026
for Khana Khazana Publications Pvt. Ltd.

(4355)
ISBN 978-81-7991-607-0

Design: Mahendra Ghanekar, Anjali Sawant

Food Styling & Photography: Swapnil Naik

Printed in India
by Thomson Press (I) Ltd.
New Delhi

AUTHOR'S NOTE

The idea of coming out with this book 'Fun Food for Fussy Kids' took shape as I have often been asked by worried mothers about what to, how to and when to feed their little ones, because most of them have children who make them run around in circles at meal time. I sympathise with them completely for I know how they feel... I have two growing daughters at home. They are in their teens now and a tad less fussy, but I remember during their early years how often Alyona would be at her wit's end over what to cook for breakfast, lunch or dinner so that our little darlings would eat without much fuss.

Cooking fun food for kids is not an easy task, but if your kid is fussy and picks at food, then the task becomes doubly challenging. While cooking for children one has to keep in mind the importance of a balanced diet. Growing bodies and minds need the right kind of nutrients in the right quantity in order to develop into healthy adulthood. Fortunately for us, there is a wide variety of food available today and one need not repeat any particular item often.

Though it is difficult to cook for fussy children, it can be made a lot easier if you involve them in the planning of the menu, cooking and serving. We usually think that children will not be interested in cooking. But believe me a lot of children are. And I am saying this from personal experience. At home, especially on Sundays, our daughters Rachita and Kriti tinker around in the kitchen. The golden rule is to ask them and involve them, not just instruct them. If you treat cooking as a game they will also feel happy to take part. You could also ask them for ideas about what they would like to eat. Sometimes something they have eaten at a friend's place catches their fancy and they would like you to cook something similar at home too. Once you know their preferences you can shop accordingly. And yes, take them along while shopping for these special dishes. Try this and you will see that the children will enjoy themselves thoroughly.

All the dishes in this book are meant for four portions keeping in mind that they will form a part of a menu. The portion size has been adjusted according to a child's appetite. Also the spice levels have been reduced to suit children. If you are cooking these dishes for adults, you will need to increase the quantities accordingly.

Happy cooking!

CONTENTS

BEVERAGES

CHOCO-COOKIE SHAKE

Last year while I was in California with Alyona and the girls, we tried out a cookie ice cream.
That was the inspiration for this delightful shake using ice cream with crushed cookies.
My kids love it and I am sure yours will love it too.

12 chocolate cookies

8 tablespoons chocolate sauce

3 cups chilled milk

8 scoops vanilla ice cream

1 Break the cookies into large bits. Coarsely crumble a few for decoration and place the rest in a blender.

2 Add the chocolate sauce, milk and vanilla ice cream, and blend till not too smooth.

3 Pour into four glasses. Sprinkle the reserved crumbled cookies on top and serve immediately.

ROSY SIPS

Pink and frothy – any little kid will reach out for this milk shake with jewelled jelly shapes floating on top. I made this drink for my younger daughter Kriti's second birthday party, and the toddlers scooped the jelly up with their tiny fingers! And then, begged for more!

3 cups chilled milk

8 tablespoons rose syrup

8 scoops butterscotch ice cream

Sugar to taste

1 cup prepared strawberry jelly

1 Set the jelly in a shallow pan and cut out tiny shapes with cocktail cookie cutters. Keep chilled.

2 Blend the chilled milk with six tablespoons of rose syrup, four scoops of ice cream and sugar to taste in a blender.

3 Pour the milk mixture into four glasses and add a few pieces of jelly to each glass.

4 Top with a scoop of ice cream and drizzle with some of the remaining rose syrup. Serve immediately.

MANGO SLURPY

The chilled mango is the secret to making this smoothie icy cold without adding ice!

3 large ripe mangoes, peeled and chopped

1 medium ripe mango, cut into ½-inch cubes or thin slices to decorate

3 cups chilled milk

6 tablespoons chilled yogurt

8 tablespoons sugar

8 tablespoons strawberry crush (optional)

10-12 ice cubes, crushed

1 Place the chopped mangoes in an airtight container in the freezer for a while.

2 Blend the chilled mangoes, milk, yogurt, sugar and crushed ice cubes together in a blender.

3 Line four glasses with the strawberry crush, if desired. Carefully pour the mixture into the prepared glasses.

4 Serve chilled, decorated with the mango cubes or slices.

STRAWBERRY MILK SHAKE

What yummier combo than a shake and a burger! Serve this with the Chicken Burger (page 52)
and come up a winner! Your kid won't miss the less than healthy fizzy drink either!

4 strawberries, sliced into fans

9 tablespoons strawberry crush

3 cups milk, chilled

8 scoops vanilla ice cream

4 tablespoons whipped cream

1 Place the milk, ice cream and eight tablespoons of strawberry crush in a blender and blend till smooth. Pour into four tall glasses.

2 Put the whipped cream into an icing bag fitted with a star nozzle and pipe a dollop of cream on top of the milk shake in each glass.

3 Drizzle some of the remaining strawberry crush over the cream. Decorate with the strawberry fans and serve immediately.

Chef's Tips:
▶Use fresh strawberries when in season instead of the strawberry crush.
▶To decorate, you can also make a small slit at the bottom of each strawberry and fix it onto the rim of each glass just before serving.

NRG MILK SHAKE

The chickoo milk shake at a popular juice centre is the inspiration here.
Dates and almonds provide the energy and nutrition that every growing child needs.

4 cups chilled milk

4 *chickoo*, peeled and chopped

8-10 seedless dates, chopped

2 tablespoons sugar

4-5 almonds, blanched, peeled and slivered

1 Place the milk, *chickoo*, dates and sugar in a blender and blend till smooth.

2 Pour into tall glasses, sprinkle with the almond slivers and serve immediately.

MELON MAGIC

Which kid can resist a drink with cool looks and great taste?
Add a fancy stirrer or colourful drinking straw to seal the deal.

1 medium ripe musk melon, cubed

2 cups fresh orange juice

2 tablespoons lemon juice

2 tablespoons honey

12-16 ice cubes, crushed

1 Place the crushed ice cubes in a blender and add the melon. Pour in the orange juice, lemon juice and honey. Blend till slushy.

2 Pour into four chilled glasses and serve immediately.

TIRAMISÙ MILK SHAKE

*This is my kiddy version of the grown-up tiramisù. Cold coffee was comfort food for me while
I was growing up. Then we started adding scoops of ice cream to make it a little
more exciting. This is cold coffee with a gooey chocolate twist!*

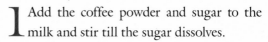

3 cups chilled milk

2 teaspoons instant coffee powder

4 teaspoons sugar

8 tablespoons chocolate sauce

1 cup whipped cream

4 chocolate chip cookies, crushed

1 Add the coffee powder and sugar to the milk and stir till the sugar dissolves.

2 Pour two tablespoons of chocolate sauce into each glass.

3 Pour half a cup of the milk mixture over the sauce.

4 Put the whipped cream into a piping bag with a star nozzle and pipe cream rosettes on top of the milk in each glass.

5 Sprinkle with the crushed cookies and serve immediately.

VEGETARIAN
TIFFINS & SNACKS

FLYING SAUCERS

My sister-in-law Jyotsna made this especially for my daughters when they spent a summer vacation with her. To provide an instant meal to a horde of hungry kids, she hit upon the idea of using tinned baked beans as a substitute for pizza sauce with toppings! Drops of Tabasco sauce will give the pizza some added zing!

1 cup tinned baked beans

8 four-inch baby wholewheat pizza breads

8 teaspoons butter

4 tablespoons Green Chutney (page 102)

1½ cups grated mozzarella cheese

Tomato ketchup, as required

1 Spread the butter on each pizza bread. Top with an even layer of green chutney.

2 Spoon some baked beans onto each pizza. Top generously with grated mozzarella cheese.

3 Place under a hot grill till the cheese melts and starts bubbling.

4 Cut into halves and serve with tomato ketchup.

SPROUT 'N' ROLL

This is a version of the puzzling Tomato 'Omelette' one finds on an Udipi vegetarian menu card!
Far from being an egg dish, it is actually a vegetarian pancake made with gram flour and tomatoes,
similar to besan ke poodey, from the North or cheela from the West. A healthy, tasty recipe for growing kids.

Batter

1½ cups gram flour

2 green chillies, optional

½ teaspoon red chilli powder

¼ teaspoon turmeric powder

¼ teaspoon carom seeds

3 tablespoons yogurt

1 tablespoon chopped fresh coriander

Salt to taste

Oil for shallow-frying

Butter, to serve

Filling

1 cup sprouted green gram, blanched

1 tablespoon oil

2 medium onions, chopped

2 medium tomatoes, seeded and chopped

1 green chilli, chopped

¼ teaspoon turmeric powder

¼ teaspoon red chilli powder

½ teaspoon *chaat masala*

Salt to taste

1 teaspoon lemon juice

1 tablespoon chopped fresh coriander

1 For the batter, mix together the gram flour, green chillies, chilli powder, turmeric powder, carom seeds, yogurt, chopped coriander and salt.

2 Add one and one-fourth cups of water and whisk to make a smooth batter of pouring consistency. Rest the batter for about fifteen minutes.

3 To make the filling, heat the oil in a non-stick pan; add the onions and tomatoes and sauté for two minutes. Add the green chilli and sprouts and continue to sauté for half a minute.

4 Add the turmeric and chilli powder, *chaat masala*, salt, lemon juice and chopped coriander, and sauté for one minute. Remove from heat and set aside.

5 Heat a non-stick *tawa*, grease it with a little oil and pour a little batter onto it. Spread into a thin round with the back of the ladle and cook till golden brown on both sides.

6 Place some stuffing in the centre and roll up. Serve hot with a dollop of butter.

CHINESE DOSA

Kids and noodles have a magnetic attraction for each other.
If making dosa is not your forte, pack the noodle stuffing into thin roti and serve.
The look of divine pleasure on your kids' faces is worth all the effort!

2 cups ready-made *dosa* batter

Oil, as required

Filling

2 teaspoons oil

5-6 garlic cloves, chopped

½ medium green capsicum, cut into thin strips

½ medium yellow capsicum, cut into thin strips

½ medium red capsicum, cut into thin strips

1 cup boiled noodles

½ teaspoon soy sauce

1 teaspoon red chilli sauce

2 tablespoons tomato ketchup

Salt to taste

Black pepper powder to taste

2 spring onions with greens, chopped

1 To make the filling, heat the oil in a non-stick pan. Add the garlic and sauté for half a minute. Add all the capsicums and sauté for a couple of minutes.

2 Add the noodles, soy sauce, chilli sauce and tomato ketchup, and toss to mix. Add the salt and pepper powder, and toss again. Sprinkle the spring onions with greens and mix again. Set aside.

3 Heat a non-stick *dosa tawa*, season with oil and wipe with a wet cloth.

4 Pour a ladleful of *dosa* batter on the *tawa* and spread it in a circular motion with the back of the ladle. Drizzle oil all around and cook for a minute.

5 Place a small portion of the filling on one half of the *dosa*. Fold the other half over and press down lightly. Serve hot.

POTATO SURPRISE

I prefer making these crisp potato delights when I have the time to properly fill and shape the croquettes. No way can you make them in a hurry. Enjoy your kid's surprised delight when they discover the melted cheese inside.

3 medium potatoes, boiled and mashed

½ cup chopped fresh coriander

½ teaspoon green chilli paste

1 teaspoon lemon juice

½ teaspoon roasted cumin powder

½ cup roasted peanuts, crushed

Salt to taste

35 grams mozzarella cheese, cut into 16 sticks

3 tablespoons refined flour

Oil for deep-frying

1/3 cup beaten rice

Date and Tamarind Chutney (page 102) or tomato ketchup, as required

1 Mix together the potatoes, fresh coriander, green chilli paste, lemon juice, cumin powder, peanuts and salt.

2 Divide the mixture into sixteen portions and shape into oval croquettes. Stuff each croquette with a mozzarella stick, making sure that the cheese is completely enclosed.

3 Mix the refined flour with half a cup of water to make a smooth batter.

4 Heat sufficient oil in a non-stick *kadai*. Dip each croquette in the batter, roll in the beaten rice and deep-fry till golden brown. Drain on absorbent paper.

5 Serve hot with the date and tamarind chutney or tomato ketchup.

CHANA PURI

Chana Puri is a typical breakfast combination in the North, and needs a little bit of hot halwa on the side to complete the triangle! It is our favourite Sunday brunch! The chana rolled up in the puri and wrapped in foil, makes a perfect tiffin snack too.

¾ cup split Bengal gram, soaked overnight

1 inch ginger

2-3 garlic cloves

Salt to taste

1 tablespoon coriander powder

1 tablespoon cumin powder

1 teaspoon red chilli powder

¼ teaspoon turmeric powder

¼ teaspoon dried mango powder

1 tablespoon cumin seeds

½ tablespoon dried pomegranate seeds

1½ tablespoons oil

2 green chillies, slit

1 medium tomato, quartered

½ teaspoon *garam masala* powder

Puri

1 cup wholewheat flour

2 tablespoons semolina

Salt to taste

Oil for deep-frying

1. Pound the ginger and garlic to a fine paste.

2. Drain the split Bengal gram, add two and half cups of water and salt, and cook till tender. Drain and reserve the cooking liquid.

3. Mix together the coriander, cumin, chilli, turmeric and dried mango powders. Dry-roast the cumin seeds and dried pomegranate seeds separately. Cool and grind the seeds together to a powder. Mix together with the rest of the spice powders.

4. Heat one tablespoon of oil in a non-stick *kadai*. Add the green chillies and ginger-garlic paste and stir-fry for a few seconds. Add the mixed spice powder and stir-fry for half a minute. Stir in one-fourth cup of the reserved cooking liquid and cook for two minutes.

5. Add the cooked gram, salt and half a cup of the reserved cooking liquid and cook on high heat for three to four minutes, stirring occasionally. Add the tomato and sprinkle *garam masala* powder and roasted pomegranate seed-cumin seed powder.

6. Heat the remaining oil and pour over the prepared gram. Stir well and adjust the seasoning.

7. For the *puri*, knead the flour and semolina with salt and enough water to make a semi-

soft dough. Cover with a damp cloth and rest the dough for half an hour.

8 Divide the dough into twelve equal portions and roll out each portion into a *puri*.

9 Heat sufficient oil in a non-stick *kadai* and deep-fry the *puri* on medium heat till golden. Drain on absorbent paper. Serve hot with the *chana*.

DIPPY STICKS

This party hit allows you to make a tub of cheese spread go a really long way!

¾ cup cheese spread

1 teaspoon cornflour

1 cup milk

1 tablespoon butter

½ medium onion, chopped

Salt to taste

½ teaspoon red chilli powder

¼ teaspoon dried oregano

To Serve

2 medium carrots, cut into fingers

2 medium cucumbers, cut into fingers

2 bread sticks, broken into 2-inch pieces

1 Mix the cornflour with one tablespoon of cold milk.

2 Heat the butter in a non-stick pan; add the onion and sauté for two minutes or till translucent.

3 Add the remaining milk, cheese spread, cornflour mixture and salt, and mix well. Bring the mixture to a boil and cook, stirring continuously, till smooth and thick. Stir in the chilli powder and oregano.

4 Remove from heat and serve immediately with the vegetable fingers and bread sticks.

CORN PANZZA

*This pan pizza is the answer to the harried mom's prayers when the grill refuses to heat up, but the cries
for pizza reach a crescendo! Yes, you can make any sort of pizza with a ready-made base in a pan.
Use a good quality thick-bottomed non-stick frying pan with a lid and you can't go wrong!
Get imaginative with the toppings and you will come out a winner.*

4 four-inch wholewheat pizza breads

2 tablespoons olive oil

Tomato Sauce

2 medium tomatoes, puréed

4 tablespoons tomato ketchup

1 tablespoon olive oil

2 garlic cloves, chopped

1 small onion, chopped

Salt to taste

½ teaspoon sugar

6-8 black peppercorns, crushed

1 teaspoon oregano

Topping

1½ cups blanched American corn kernels

4-5 black peppercorns, crushed

2 cups grated mozzarella cheese

1 For the tomato sauce, heat the oil in a non-stick pan; add the garlic and sauté for half a minute. Add the onion and sauté till translucent.

2 Stir in the tomato purée and cook till thick. Add the tomato ketchup and cook for another five to eight minutes.

3 Add the salt, sugar, crushed peppercorns and oregano, and mix well. Set aside to cool.

4 Heat half a tablespoon of olive oil in a non-stick pan and place a pizza base on it. Spread a quarter of the tomato sauce evenly on the pizza. Scatter one-fourth of the corn over the sauce and sprinkle the crushed peppercorns. Top with one-fourth of the grated cheese.

5 Cover the pan with a lid and cook on very low heat for ten minutes, or till the base has evenly browned and the cheese has melted. Cut into wedges and serve hot.

Chef's Tip:
For younger children you can serve half a pizza per child or use baby pizza breads.

NRG DOSA

This recipe does not require much energy to make, but it will definitely energise you when you eat it! Simply put, the batter is power-packed with a variety of flours, and according to my colleague Neena, we should keep the ingredients a secret as, she says, kids may balk at eating nachni, soya or bajra flour. She used this trick on her unsuspecting son and he used to polish off one dosa after another!

¼ cup rice flour

¼ cup wheat flour

¼ cup soya flour

¼ cup finger millet flour

Buttermilk as required

Salt to taste

2 tablespoons chopped fresh coriander

2 green chillies, chopped

Oil for shallow-frying

Tomato ketchup, as required

1 Mix together the rice, wheat, soya and millet flour with the buttermilk to make a smooth batter.

2 Add the salt, chopped coriander and green chillies, and mix well. Let the batter rest for about fifteen minutes.

3 Heat a thick non-stick *tawa* or frying pan. Add two drops of oil and wipe the *tawa* clean with a piece of wet muslin.

4 Add a tablespoon of oil to the *tawa*; pour half a ladleful of batter and spread it to a thin three-inch round.

5 Drizzle a little oil all around. When the underside is cooked, flip the *dosa* and fry the other side. Serve hot with tomato ketchup.

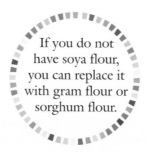
If you do not have soya flour, you can replace it with gram flour or sorghum flour.

COCKTAIL IDLI

While I was finalising this recipe, Alyona came up with an objection ... why use the word 'cocktail' in a book on food for kids? Point taken, but the fact remains that this recipe is perfect for a kid's party - the tasty tidbits will wow the grown-ups too!

1 cup parboiled rice

½ cup skinless split black gram

Salt to taste

1 large onion, cut into 1-inch cubes, layers separated

1 large green capsicum, cut into 1-inch pieces

1 large tomato, seeded and cut into 1-inch pieces

2 tablespoons oil

2 tablespoons tomato ketchup

1 tablespoon red chilli sauce

12 toothpicks

Rasam, as required

1 Wash the rice and soak in three cups of water for at least two to three hours.

2 Wash and soak the split black gram in two cups of water for a similar length of time.

3 Drain and grind the rice to a slightly coarse texture. Add enough water to make a batter of dropping consistency. Drain and grind the split black gram, sprinkling water as required to a make a smooth, spongy batter.

4 Mix both the batters together. Add salt and mix thoroughly in a whipping motion with your hand. Pour the batter into a large container, close tightly with a lid and leave to stand in a warm place overnight or for at least six hours.

5 Heat sufficient water in a steamer. Place a piece of wet muslin on the moulds of a mini *idli* stand. Pour a spoonful of the fermented batter into each mould.

6 Place the *idli* stand in the steamer. Cook for eight to ten minutes or till the *idli* are done. Remove the *idli* from the moulds.

7 Thread the *idli* and vegetables onto each toothpick in the following order: onion, *idli*, capsicum, *idli*, tomato.

8 Heat the oil in a non-stick pan and arrange the toothpicks on it. Add the tomato ketchup and chilli sauce and toss to coat the *idli* with the sauce.

9 Serve the *idli* with the *rasam*. Pour a little *rasam* into small glasses, place the toothpicks across the rims.

10 Serve immediately.

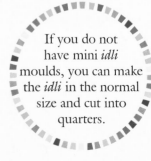

If you do not have mini *idli* moulds, you can make the *idli* in the normal size and cut into quarters.

COLESLAW TACOS

Any cook in a hurry would prefer to mix up the cut veggies into the mayonnaise sauce, right? But the overall effect of serving the two separately in a delicate taco shell is more fun, and has more colour and texture. Brown bread sandwiches with the coleslaw filling are perfect for picnics too.

12 ready-made tacos shells

¼ medium cabbage, shredded

1 medium carrot, grated

1 small yellow capsicum, cut into thin strips

1 small red capsicum, cut into thin strips

1 small green capsicum, gut into thin strips

50 grams cottage cheese, cut into small cubes

Salt to taste

Black pepper powder to taste

¼ cup Eggless Mayonnaise (page 102)

¼ cup cream cheese

2 tablespoons tomato ketchup

4 spring onions, cut into thin strips

1 Mix together the cabbage, carrot, yellow, red and green capsicums, cottage cheese, salt and pepper powder in a bowl.

2 Mix together the mayonnaise, cream cheese and tomato ketchup in another bowl.

3 Place a tablespoonful of the vegetable mixture into each taco shell, drizzle a little of the mayonnaise mixture over and garnish with the spring onions.

4 Serve immediately.

MASALA POTATO WEDGES

It's so easy to bring home a pack of frozen potato wedges and fry them in the blink of an eye. But, if this food is such a favourite why not make it healthier? Make the wedges as chatpata as you can and far away from the deep-frier!

6 medium potatoes, cut into 8 wedges each

Salt to taste

½ cup refined flour

¼ teaspoon black pepper powder

3 tablespoons oil

Spice Mix

½ teaspoon mixed dried herbs

¼ teaspoon red chilli flakes

½ teaspoon *chaat masala*

1 Preheat an oven to 180°C/350°F/Gas Mark 4.

2 Parboil the potato wedges in salted water. Drain, pat dry and set aside to cool.

3 Mix together the refined flour, salt and pepper powder. Toss the potato wedges in the mixture.

4 Place the wedges on a greased baking tray, drizzle the oil over and bake in the preheated oven for fifteen to twenty minutes.

5 Mix together the mixed herbs, chilli flakes and *chaat masala,* and sprinkle over the wedges. Serve hot.

Chef's Tip:
Potato wedges tend to get soggy, so serve immediately.

NAUGHTY 'N' NICE NACHOS

I think it is an excellent idea to be able to make tortilla chips in large quantities at home for sudden snack attacks! Another quick fix idea: just top the chips with grated cheese and baked beans and heat in a microwave oven on HIGH (100%) for a few seconds. Sprinkle with red chilli flakes, and in no time will you be handed the empty plate back for a refill.

¼ cup maize flour

¼ cup refined flour + for dusting

1 teaspoon oil + for deep-frying

Salt to taste

Cheese Sauce

½ cup grated processed cheese

1 tablespoon oil

6-8 garlic cloves, crushed

½ cup White Sauce (page 102)

½ teaspoon white pepper powder

Salsa

5 medium tomatoes, halved

1 tablespoon oil

2 onions, chopped

1 green chilli, chopped

1 teaspoon vinegar

Salt to taste

¼ teaspoon black pepper powder

2 tablespoons chopped fresh coriander

Chef's Tip:
For a quicker, colourful topping, instead of the salsa, sprinkle finely chopped green, red and yellow capsicums on top of the cheese sauce.

1 Mix together the maize flour, refined flour, one teaspoon oil and salt in a bowl. Add sufficient hot water and knead into a soft dough.

2 Divide the dough into six equal portions and roll into balls. Dust the balls with flour and roll out into thin *chapati*. Cut each *chapati* into four triangles.

3 Heat sufficient oil in a deep non-stick pan and deep-fry the triangles on low heat till crisp. Drain on absorbent paper and set aside to cool.

4 To prepare the cheese sauce, heat the oil in a non-stick pan. Add the garlic and sauté for a few seconds. Stir in the white sauce, add the white pepper powder and cheese, and stir to mix.

5 For the salsa, heat a non-stick pan and roast the tomatoes till the skins char. Cool and peel. Chop two tomatoes and purée the rest.

6 Heat the oil in a non-stick pan and sauté the onions and green chilli for two minutes. Add the tomatoes, tomato purée, vinegar, salt and pepper powder, and cook for two minutes. Take the pan off the heat and set aside to cool. Stir in the chopped coriander.

7 To serve, arrange the tortilla chips on a plate, spread a little cheese sauce over them and top with the salsa. Serve immediately.

EASY-PEASY TIKKI

During the recipe trials some of my colleagues doubted that the broken wheat would hold together while frying. Well, I knew all along that the green peas would be the binding material! This is an excellent way to feed two nutritious foods like wheat and peas to fussy kids without them catching on!

½ cup broken wheat

1 cup shelled green peas

1 green chilli, chopped

2 teaspoons *chaat masala*

½ cup chopped fresh coriander

2 tablespoons lemon juice

6 garlic cloves, chopped

Salt to taste

Cornflour for dusting

3 tablespoons oil

Green Chutney (page 102) or tomato ketchup, as required

1 Soak the broken wheat in one cup of hot water for half an hour. Drain and put it into a food processor or blender.

2 Add the green peas, green chilli, *chaat masala*, chopped coriander, lemon juice, garlic and salt, and grind together.

3 Transfer the mixture to a bowl. Divide into sixteen equal portions and shape each one into a *tikki*.

4 Heat sufficient oil in a non-stick *kadai* and deep-fry the *tikki* till golden brown.

5 Drain on absorbent paper. Serve hot with green chutney or tomato ketchup.

You can also shallow-fry the *tikki* for a healthier option.

TAN-TANA-TAN TOAST

*Boiled moong is a low-fat, high-protein natural food that is good for the whole family.
I sometimes add chopped cucumber, tomato and spring onions, a dash of lemon and salt, and
eat it as a salad. These toasts with moong topping are Alyona's Mom's creation, so all the
credit should go to her! Just don't forget the ketchup!*

1 cup whole green gram, soaked

8 brown bread slices

Salt to taste

2 tablespoons oil

1 bay leaf

3-4 cloves

½ teaspoon cumin seeds

12 curry leaves

½ teaspoon turmeric powder

½ teaspoon red chilli powder

1 tablespoon chopped fresh coriander

Butter as required

Tomato ketchup, as required

Chef's Tip:
You can use the reserved moong stock in a soup,
or to knead wholewheat flour to make *roti*.
Healthy and tasty!

1 Boil the whole green gram in five cups of water and salt in a deep non-stick pan. When the water begins to boil, lower the heat and simmer until the gram is completely cooked and soft. You can also pressure-cook the gram till the pressure is released four times (four whistles). Drain and reserve the stock for use in some other recipe.

2 Heat the oil in a non-stick pan; add the bay leaf and cloves and sauté for a couple of seconds. Add the cumin seeds, and when they begin to change colour, add the curry leaves and sauté for a few seconds.

3 Add the turmeric powder and chilli powder, and stir again. Add the boiled green gram and salt, if required, and cook for two minutes. Add the chopped coriander and mix well.

4 Spread the butter on one side of all the bread slices. Place four slices on the worktop and spread the green gram mixture evenly on them. Cover each topped slice with another slice, buttered side down.

5 Spread a little butter on the outer surfaces of the sandwiches and grill or toast them in a sandwich toaster till crisp and golden on both sides. Serve immediately with tomato ketchup.

PANEER KRISPIES

I must confess that this recipe is inspired by the paneer pakore of Lawrence Road in Amritsar. There are few things more satisfying to the palate than soft paneer enclosed in a crispy crust.

200 grams cottage cheese

2 tablespoons tomato sauce

2 teaspoons red chilli sauce

¼ cup cornflour

½ cup refined flour

A pinch of soda bicarbonate

Salt to taste

Milk as required

Oil for deep-frying

Tomato ketchup, as required

1 Cut the cottage cheese into twenty long fingers or forty small fingers. Mix together the tomato sauce and chilli sauce, and marinate the cottage cheese fingers in the mixture for fifteen minutes.

2 Mix together the cornflour, refined flour, soda bicarbonate, salt and sufficient milk to make a moderately thick batter. Rest the batter for fifteen minutes.

3 Heat sufficient oil in a non-stick *kadai*, dip the cottage cheese fingers in the batter and deep-fry till golden.

4 Drain on absorbent paper. Serve hot with tomato ketchup.

PAV BHAJI BUNS

The sandwich had its origin in Portsmouth in England hundreds of years ago. It was invented because the Earl of Sandwich wanted food which he could eat using one hand while he played cards with the other! Well, sandwiches have come a long way since then and I have invented this version so that eating pav bhaji can be less messy for our little lords and ladies at home.

8 wholewheat *pav*

3 tablespoons butter + for shallow-frying

2 tablespoons oil

2 medium onions, chopped

1 green chilli, chopped

1 tablespoon ginger-garlic paste

3 medium tomatoes, chopped

1 medium green capsicum, chopped

¼ cup shelled green peas, blanched and mashed

4 medium potatoes, boiled and grated

1½ tablespoons *pav bhaji masala*

Salt to taste

1 tablespoon chopped fresh coriander

1 tablespoon lemon juice

1 Heat two tablespoons of butter and the oil in a non-stick pan; add three-fourth of the onions and sauté till light golden brown. Add the green chilli and ginger-garlic paste, and sauté for half a minute.

2 Add half the tomatoes and cook on medium heat, stirring continuously, for three to four minutes, or till the oil separates from the *masala*.

3 Add the capsicum, green peas, potatoes and one cup of water. Bring to a boil and simmer for ten minutes, pressing down with the back of the spoon a few times, till all the vegetables are completely mashed.

4 Add the *pav bhaji masala*, salt and the remaining tomatoes. Cook on medium heat, stirring continuously, for two minutes or till the mixture is thick and of spreading consistency. Add the chopped coriander, lemon juice and one tablespoon of butter, and remove from heat. Allow to cool slightly.

5 Slit the *pav* without cutting through. Spread some of the vegetable mixture on the lower half. Spread some butter on both the outer surfaces of the *pav*.

6 Heat a flat non-stick *tawa* and cook the *pav* on low heat till golden and crisp on the outside. Serve hot.

TRI-COLOUR SANDWICHES

Perfect for Republic Day and Independence Day celebrations! Pack the kids' dabba to the brim because the very sight of these sandwiches is mouthwatering! And you can be sure they'll be demanding more helpings of these colourful sandwiches, and so will their friends!

8 brown bread slices

4 white bread slices

Orange Layer

1 cup grated carrots

2 tablespoons Eggless Mayonnaise (page 102)

Salt to taste

Green Layer

1 cup grated cottage cheese

4 tablespoons Green Chutney (page 102)

Salt to taste

1 For the orange layer, mix together the carrots, eggless mayonnaise and salt.

2 For the green layer, mix together the cottage cheese with the green chutney and salt.

3 Place a slice of brown bread on the worktop. Spread the green layer evenly over it. Place a slice of white bread over it.

4 Spread the orange layer evenly over the white bread and cover with a slice of brown bread. Press down gently. Cut each sandwich into three fingers and serve at once, or pack into tiffin boxes.

PANCAKE TRIANGLES

Pancakes do not have to be sweet. Honey and maple syrup can take a break while we roll them around a spicy corn filling. If you make the batter a little thick, you can make small round pancakes and then top with the filling to produce pretty little mouthfuls.

Pancakes

⅓ cup refined flour

⅓ cup wholewheat flour

1 teaspoon baking powder

Salt to taste

1½ cups milk

4 teaspoons oil for shallow-frying

Filling

1 teaspoon butter

2 spring onions, chopped

2 green capsicums, chopped

¾ cup sweetcorn kernels, cooked

Salt to taste

¼ teaspoon black pepper powder

¼ teaspoon mustard paste

1 tablespoon tomato ketchup

1 For the pancakes, sift the flours with the baking powder and salt into a deep bowl. Add the milk and whisk well to prevent lumps from forming. Let the batter rest for ten minutes.

2 For the filling, heat the butter in a non-stick pan. Add the spring onions and sauté for one minute.

3 Add the capsicums, corn, salt, pepper powder and mustard paste, and sauté for one minute. Remove from heat and stir in the tomato ketchup. Set aside.

4 For each pancake, heat one teaspoon of oil in a six-inch non-stick frying pan. Pour a ladleful of the batter and swirl the pan so that the batter spreads evenly around. Cook till the underside is lightly browned. Cook only on one side and remove.

5 Place each pancake, with the cooked side down, on a flat surface and cut in half. Spoon a portion of the stuffing on one side of each half and fold over the other side to make a triangle. Press the edges down well.

6 Serve immediately.

PANEER FRANKIES

Frankly speaking, frankies are an excellent way to feed sabzi roti to kids!
Frankies can be made with aloo sabzi, egg bhurji, and just plain chopped salad....
like I said, give your imagination free reign.

150 grams cottage cheese, crumbled

1 cup wholewheat flour

Salt to taste

1 tablespoon oil + for shallow-frying

1 large onion, roughly chopped

1 large tomato, chopped

1 teaspoon ginger paste

1 teaspoon garlic paste

¼ teaspoon Kashmiri chilli powder

¼ teaspoon turmeric powder

1 teaspoon coriander powder (optional)

1 tablespoon lemon juice

4 teaspoons Green Chutney (page 102)

1 medium onion, finely chopped

Chaat masala, as required

1 Mix together the wholewheat flour and salt, with sufficient water and knead into a firm dough. Cover with a damp cloth and set aside for about fifteen minutes.

2 Heat the oil in a non-stick pan; add the onion, tomato, ginger paste, garlic paste, salt, chilli powder, turmeric powder and coriander powder, and stir well. Cook till soft and pulpy and the excess moisture has dried up.

3 Add the cottage cheese and lemon juice; stir and take the pan off the heat. Divide the filling into four equal portions and set aside.

4 Divide the dough into four equal balls and roll out into thin *roti*.

5 Heat a non-stick *tawa*, place a *roti* on it, drizzle a little oil all around and cook till both sides are evenly cooked.

6 Spread a teaspoon of green chutney over each *roti*. Place a portion of cottage cheese mixture at one end. Sprinkle some onion and *chaat masala* over the filling and roll up the *roti*.

7 Wrap in aluminum foil or greaseproof paper and serve.

For a non-vegetarian version, replace cottage cheese with boneless chicken cubes. Add the chicken to the onion-tomato *masala* and cook till tender.

NON-VEGETARIAN TIFFINS & SNACKS

CHEESE 'WICHES

*These cheesy French toast sandwiches are filling and great for a late
Sunday breakfast when you know lunch is a few hours away;
or for on demand snacks guaranteed to keep those tantrums at bay!*

4 cheese slices

8 brown bread slices

4 tablespoons butter

4 tablespoons tomato ketchup + for serving

2 eggs, beaten

½ cup milk

2 teaspoons sugar

Salt to taste

Black pepper powder to taste

2 tablespoons olive oil

1 Spread the butter and tomato ketchup on the bread slices.

2 Place the cheese slices on four bread slices and cover with the remaining bread. Trim the edge and cut each sandwich diagonally into two triangles.

3 Add the milk, sugar, salt and pepper powder to the beaten eggs, and whisk well.

4 Heat the olive oil in a non-stick pan. Dip each sandwich in the egg mixture and place on the pan. Cook till evenly golden brown on both sides.

5 Serve hot with tomato ketchup.

CHICKEN BASKETS

These canapés are perfect for little mouths too, as they are bite-sized and crunchy, with a smooth, creamy filling. No opportunity here for that whiny 'isme mirchi hai' fuss as an excuse to avoid eating!

2 (150 grams each) boneless chicken breasts, boiled and chopped

20 ready-made canapé cases

2 tablespoons butter

3 garlic cloves, chopped

2 medium onions, chopped

¼ cup White Sauce (page 102)

2 tablespoons grated processed cheese

Salt to taste

2 teaspoons black pepper powder

1 Grill the canapé shells in the grill mode of a microwave oven for three to five minutes, or until crisp and golden brown. Set aside.

2 Heat the butter in a non-stick pan; add the garlic and onions, and sauté for two to three minutes. Add the chicken and sauté for another two minutes.

3 Add the white sauce and cook for two minutes. Add the cheese, salt and pepper, and mix well. Set aside to cool slightly.

4 Fill the canapé shells with the chicken mixture and serve immediately.

CHICKEN POPS

Top of the pops! And, they've got cheese too, so kids will wolf them down.

2 (250 grams) boneless chicken breasts, cut into 2-inch long pieces

1 teaspoon ginger paste

1 teaspoon garlic paste

1 tablespoon chopped fresh coriander

¼ teaspoon white pepper powder

Salt to taste

50 grams processed cheese, cut into 1-inch long sticks

Oil for deep-frying

1 egg, beaten

¾ cup breadcrumbs

Green Chutney (page 102), as required

1 Slit each piece of chicken and open it up.

2 For the marinade, mix together the ginger and garlic pastes, chopped coriander, white pepper powder and salt in a bowl. Marinate the chicken pieces in the mixture for ten minutes.

3 Place a cheese stick on each piece of chicken and roll up the chicken to cover the cheese.

4 Heat sufficient oil in a non-stick *kadai*. Dip each chicken roll in the beaten egg, coat with the breadcrumbs and deep-fry till crisp and golden. Drain on absorbent paper and serve hot with green chutney.

CHICKEN BURRITOS

This is a do-it-yourself snack that will delight the fussiest kid! It's so easy, even our younger daughter, Kriti, can put it together in a jiffy, which she does willingly for us all! The burritos can be assembled while watching a movie...so the kids are happy and the adults are too!

4 wholewheat tortillas

4 tablespoons Salsa (page 102)

Filling

250 grams boneless chicken, cut into long strips

½ tablespoon soy sauce

½ tablespoon vinegar

¼ teaspoon red chilli flakes

Salt to taste

3 tablespoons oil

3-4 garlic cloves, chopped

½ small green capsicum, cut into strips

1 spring onion, chopped diagonally

1 For the filling, marinate the chicken in a mixture of soy sauce, vinegar, chilli flakes and salt for half an hour.

2 Heat the oil in a non-stick pan; add the garlic and sauté for half a minute. Add the marinated chicken, capsicum and spring onion, and cook on medium heat till the chicken is tender. Check the seasonings and remove from the heat. Divide the mixture into four portions.

3 When ready to serve, warm the tortillas and spread a tablespoon of salsa over each one. Spread a portion of the hot chicken mixture at one end and roll up the tortillas. Serve immediately.

Chef's Tip:
Use leftover cooked shredded chicken, stir-fried with the sauces, spices and vegetables for a speedier snack.

CHICKEN BURGERS

Junk food can be nutritious too! I have added soya to increase the protein in this snack. If your kids are always on the move, it will sustain them through homework and play time!

½ cup minced chicken

½ cup soya chunks

4 wholewheat buns

¾ cup warm milk

Salt to taste

¼ teaspoon black pepper powder

1 medium onion, chopped

4 garlic cloves, chopped

1 inch ginger, chopped

Oil for shallow-frying

4 lettuce leaves

2 medium tomatoes, cut into round slices

Sauce

1 tablespoon oil

1 inch ginger, grated

1 cup orange juice

1 tablespoon brown sugar

Salt to taste

1 teaspoon dark soy sauce

¼ cup tomato purée

½ teaspoon red chilli powder

1 tablespoon cornflour

1 Soak the soya chunks in the warm milk. Place the minced chicken in a grinder. Drain the soya chunks and squeeze to remove excess milk; add to the chicken in the grinder.

2 Add the salt, pepper powder, onion, garlic and ginger, and grind till smooth. Divide the chicken mixture into four equal portions and shape with moistened hands into round patties.

3 Heat the oil in a non-stick pan and shallow-fry the patties on both sides till golden brown. Drain on absorbent paper.

4 For the sauce, heat the oil in a non-stick pan; add the ginger and sauté for half a minute. Stir in the orange juice, brown sugar, salt and soy sauce, and cook till the mixture reduces slightly.

5 Add the tomato purée and chilli powder, and mix. Simmer till it reduces a little more. Add the cornflour mixed in a little water and stir till the sauce thickens.

6 Slice the buns horizontally into two. Toast lightly. Place a lettuce leaf on one half and top with two tomato slices. Place a chicken burger on top and cover with the other half of the bun. Serve immediately with the sauce.

Chef's Tip:
You can roll the patties in breadcrumbs and freeze them in an airtight bag or container. Just before serving, take them out of the freezer and shallow-fry till golden brown.

HEARTY BITES

I chose to make these tikki heart-shaped, because they do win kids' hearts, but any shape will do fine. Make sure you have a whole lot of these on hand when you have your kids' friends over for an impromptu snack.

2 hard-boiled eggs

½ medium onion, finely chopped

5-6 French beans, finely chopped

½ medium carrot, grated

5-6 spinach leaves, blanched and chopped

2 tablespoons grated processed cheese

1 tablespoon cornflour

½ teaspoon salt

½ teaspoon black pepper powder

½ teaspoon mustard paste

2 teaspoons tomato ketchup + to serve

1 cup fresh breadcrumbs

Oil for shallow-frying

1 Grate the boiled eggs into a bowl. Add the onion, French beans, carrot, spinach, cheese, cornflour, salt, pepper, mustard paste, tomato ketchup and breadcrumbs, and mix well.

2 Divide the mixture into eight equal portions and shape each portion into a heart-shaped *tikki*, or any other shape.

3 Heat sufficient oil in a non-stick frying pan and shallow-fry the *tikki* on medium heat till golden brown on both sides. Drain on absorbent paper.

4 Serve hot with tomato ketchup.

KEEEMA MATAR ROLLS

*This is a version of a hurried lunch I put together the other day. With too little time to eat
a proper lunch, I rolled up some keema in a roti and carried it with me to the car!
I admit it was not the healthiest way to dine, but it did give me a moment of inspiration!*

300 grams minced mutton

½ cup fresh or frozen shelled green peas

4 wholewheat flour *roti*

3 tablespoons oil

2 large onions, chopped

5 garlic cloves, chopped

½ inch ginger, grated

1 green chilli, finely chopped

1 teaspoon coriander powder

¾ teaspoon cumin powder

½ teaspoon red chilli powder

Salt to taste

½ teaspoon *garam masala* powder

2 tablespoons butter

4 teaspoons Green Chutney (page 102)

2 tablespoons tomato ketchup

2 teaspoons lemon juice

2 tablespoons chopped fresh coriander

1 tablespoon *chaat masala*

1 Heat the oil in a non-stick pan; add half the onions and sauté till lightly browned. Add the garlic and stir-fry for a minute.

2 Add the minced mutton, ginger, green chilli, coriander powder, cumin powder and chilli powder. Sauté for five minutes, breaking up any lumps.

3 Add three-fourth cup of water and bring to a boil. Cover the pan, lower the heat and simmer for half an hour.

4 Add the peas, salt, *garam masala* powder and another cup of water. Mix well and simmer, covered, for about ten minutes till the peas are cooked.

5 Spread each *roti* evenly with butter and green chutney. Spread a portion of the mutton filling on the *roti* and drizzle some tomato ketchup and lemon juice on top.

6 Sprinkle chopped coriander, the remaining onions and *chaat masala*, and roll the *roti* up tightly to enclose the filling. Wrap in aluminium foil and serve.

MACHHI MAGIC

Amazingly delicious, I am sure your entire family will love these delightful treats from the sea.
Tender and soft, this is a good way of introducing fish into a young child's diet.

300 grams king fish (*surmai*), thickly sliced

Salt to taste

3 black peppercorns

1 medium potato, boiled and mashed

2 eggs

3 garlic cloves, finely chopped

½ inch ginger, finely chopped

1 green chilli, finely chopped

1 tablespoon lemon juice

1 medium onion, finely chopped

1 tablespoon chopped fresh coriander

Breadcrumbs, as required

Oil for shallow-frying

Tomato ketchup, as required

1 Cook the fish in one cup of water with salt and peppercorns in a non-stick shallow pan, till all the water has evaporated. Leave to cool and carefully remove the skin, bones and peppercorns. Mash the fish with a fork.

2 Mix the mashed fish with the potato, one egg, the garlic, ginger, green chilli, lemon juice, onion, salt and chopped coriander.

3 Divide the mixture into eight equal portions and shape into flat, round cakes.

4 Beat the remaining egg. Dip each fish cake in the beaten egg and roll in the breadcrumbs.

5 Heat the oil in a non-stick frying pan on medium heat and shallow-fry the fish cakes till golden brown on both sides.

6 Drain on absorbent paper and serve hot with tomato ketchup.

To make prawn cutlets, replace fish with peeled, deveined prawns.

FISH STIX

This recipe is an Indianised version of the Angrezi-style fried fish, but so much more succulent.
Fish 'n' chips with tartare sauce was a real treat whenever we went out to eat at a fancy restaurant in
our childhood. My brother, Rajeev, used to add mustard sauce and tomato ketchup too!

300 grams fish (*ghol/bekti*) fillets

1 tablespoon ginger paste

1 tablespoon garlic paste

Salt to taste

2 tablespoons lemon juice

1 teaspoon red chilli powder

½ cup coarse rice flour

Oil for deep-frying

Potato wafers, to serve

Tomato ketchup, as required

1 Cut the fish fillets into three-inch by half-inch by half-inch fingers.

2 Marinate the fish fingers in a mixture of the ginger paste, garlic paste, salt and lemon juice for half an hour.

3 Mix together the salt, chilli powder and rice flour, and spread the mixture on a plate.

4 Remove the fish fingers from the marinade and roll them in the seasoned rice flour.

5 Heat the oil in a non-stick *kadai* and deep-fry the fish till cooked and crisp.

6 Drain on absorbent paper. Serve hot with potato wafers and tomato ketchup.

SCRAMBLED EGG CUP

A boiled egg served in an egg cup was a popular breakfast dish when I was a kid. But today's kids don't seem to have the time to sit and enjoy the pleasures of dipping hot buttered toast into a runny egg! All said and done, this is a fancy way of serving an egg in an edible cup!

4 eggs, beaten

4 small wholewheat burger buns

2 tablespoons oil

1 inch ginger, chopped

4 garlic cloves, chopped

1 medium onion, chopped

1 large tomato, chopped

1 teaspoon red chilli powder

Salt to taste

2 tablespoons chopped fresh coriander

2 tablespoons melted butter

4 tablespoons White Sauce (page 102)

1 Preheat an oven to 180°C/350°F/Gas Mark 4.

2 Heat the oil in a non-stick pan; add the ginger, garlic and onion, and sauté till golden. Add the tomato, chilli powder, two tablespoons of water and salt, and stir to mix.

3 Add the eggs and chopped coriander and cook, stirring continuously, till the eggs scramble. Divide the mixture into four equal portions.

4 Cut a thin slice off the top of each bun and scoop out the centre to form bread cups. Brush the melted butter on the insides of the cups and spoon one portion of the filling into each one, heaping it into a mound.

5 Drizzle a tablespoon of white sauce on top of each egg mound. Grill the buns in the preheated oven till the sauce bubbles and turns a light golden brown. Serve hot.

VEGETARIAN MEALS

MACARONI MAZAA

*Macaroni with cheese is slowly becoming a comfort food in Indian homes.
With a few additions like corn, capsicums and beans it becomes
a fairly substantial snack which could well work as a meal!*

1½ cups (200 grams) macaroni

4 tablespoons oil

Salt to taste

2 large onions, cut into ½-inch squares

½ cup tinned sweetcorn kernels

1 medium green capsicum, seeded and cut
into ½-inch square pieces

½ cup (150 grams) tinned baked beans

4 tablespoons tomato ketchup

2 teaspoons red chilli sauce

2 teaspoons soy sauce

½ cup cream

2 tablespoons grated processed cheese

1 Bring plenty of water to a boil in a pan;
add half a teaspoon of oil and a little salt
and cook the macaroni till *al dente* (cooked,
but firm to the bite). Drain and refresh in cold
water. Spread out on a plate to cool.

2 Heat the remaining oil in a non-stick pan;
add the onions and sauté till translucent.

3 Add the corn and sauté for a couple of
minutes. Add the capsicum and baked
beans, and sauté for three to four minutes.

4 Add the cooked macaroni, tomato ketchup,
chilli sauce, soy sauce and salt, and toss
gently to mix.

5 Add the cream and toss again. Sprinkle the
cheese and serve hot.

SOUPER POWER

A little effort to pretty up food goes a long way!
This soup with tomatoes and dal is undoubtedly healthy and perfect for kids.
Whet their appetites with the crisp heart-shaped croutons floating in the bowl!

4 medium-sized, ripe red tomatoes, quartered

2 tablespoons skinless split green
gram, soaked

1 tablespoon olive oil

1 small onion, sliced

1 inch ginger, sliced

2 garlic cloves, sliced

Salt to taste

1 tablespoon sugar

White pepper powder to taste

4 brown bread slices

4 fresh coriander sprigs

1 Heat the oil in a pressure cooker. Add the onion, ginger and garlic, and sauté till lightly browned.

2 Add the split green gram and sauté for a minute. Add two cups of water and bring the mixture to a boil. Add the salt, sugar and pepper powder, and stir. Add the tomatoes and mix.

3 Cover the cooker with the lid and cook under pressure till the pressure is released four times (four whistles).

4 Cut the brown bread slices into heart shapes with a cookie cutter. Heat a non-stick pan and toast the bread hearts till crisp and golden brown.

5 Strain the cooked tomato-gram mixture and reserve the stock. Blend the solids in a blender to make a smooth purée.

6 Pass the purée through a sieve into a deep non-stick pan. Stir in the strained stock and bring the mixture to a boil. Adjust the seasoning.

7 Pour the soup into four soup bowls, garnish with the bread hearts and fresh coriander sprigs, and serve hot.

TOMATO TEMPTATION

I like this recipe a lot and so do my daughters. It makes its way into their tiffin boxes at least once a fortnight. The colourful combination of vegetables and peanuts, and the delightful aroma is sure to create some excitement when the tiffin box is opened.

½ cup tomato purée

¾ cup rice, soaked

3 tablespoons oil

¼ cup peanuts

1 teaspoon cumin seeds

1 medium onion, sliced

1 teaspoon garlic paste

¾ cup bean sprouts

1 medium carrot, chopped

20 French beans, chopped

Salt to taste

½ teaspoon red chilli powder

1 tablespoon lemon juice

1 Heat the oil in a heavy-bottomed non-stick pan and add the peanuts. Fry until lightly browned. Drain and set aside.

2 Add the cumin seeds to the oil remaining in the pan and when they begin to change colour, add the onion and sauté until light brown. Add the garlic paste and sauté for one minute longer.

3 Add the bean sprouts and cook for a minute. Add the carrot and French beans, and continue to sauté for two to three minutes.

4 Stir in the tomato purée, salt and chilli powder, and cook till the mixture is quite dry.

5 Add the drained rice and stir in gently. Stir in three cups of water and bring to a boil.

6 Cover and simmer for twelve to fifteen minutes or until the water has been absorbed and the rice is cooked.

7 Mix in the fried peanuts and lemon juice, and serve hot.

CHATPATA BHINDI

Bhindi made the right way is popular with many kids, including mine.
Simply roll up a few bhindi in roti and you have a handy, healthy meal. I love it too!

200 grams small ladies' fingers

½ teaspoon turmeric powder

½ teaspoon *garam masala* powder

1 teaspoon roasted cumin powder

¼ teaspoon red chilli powder

1 tablespoon coriander powder

Salt to taste

3 teaspoons *chaat masala*

1 teaspoon fennel seeds, crushed

2 tablespoons oil

8-10 shallots

2 tablespoons gram flour

1 tablespoon chopped fresh coriander

1 teaspoon dried mango powder

1 Trim the ladies' fingers and make a slit on one side without cutting through.

2 Mix together the turmeric, *garam masala*, roasted cumin, chilli and coriander powders, salt, one teaspoon of *chaat masala* and the fennel seeds in a small bowl.

3 Fill the mixture into the slits of the ladies' fingers. Sprinkle any remaining mixture over the ladies' fingers and add a tablespoon of oil. Mix and set aside.

4 Heat the remaining oil in a non-stick *kadai*; add the shallots and sauté for one minute.

5 Add the gram flour and sauté for a couple of minutes.

6 Add the stuffed ladies' fingers and mix. Lower the heat, cover and cook, stirring occasionally, till the ladies' fingers become crisp.

7 Garnish with the chopped coriander, sprinkle the remaining *chaat masala* and dried mango powder, and serve hot.

SWEETCORN VEGETABLE SOUP

I have used a minimal amount of finely chopped vegetables, so that they mix well in the soup and are difficult to fish out! Corn is always a favourite and the rest of the vegetables get gobbled up in the process.

¼ cup sweetcorn kernels

150 grams cream-style sweetcorn

¼ small cabbage, chopped

¼ medium carrot, diced

1 tablespoon oil

4 cups Vegetable Stock (page 102)

1½ tablespoons cornflour

Salt to taste

¼ teaspoon white pepper powder

½ tablespoon sugar

1 stalk spring onion greens, chopped

1 Heat the oil in a non-stick wok or pan; add the corn kernels, cabbage and carrot, and stir-fry for a couple of minutes. Stir in the vegetable stock and bring to a boil.

2 Mix in the cream-style corn and continue cooking for two to three minutes, or until well mixed.

3 Add the salt, white pepper powder and sugar. Mix the cornflour with a quarter cup of water and stir into the mixture.

4 Cook, stirring continuously, on high heat for one minute, or until the soup thickens.

5 Serve piping hot, garnished with the spring onion greens.

PASTA JUMBLE

Fun time at the table! Pasta in different shapes and colours is appealing to little ones.
Use alphabet pasta and play the 'name-the-alphabet' game while your kid wolfs it down.
Wholewheat flour in the white sauce adds much-needed fiber.

1 cup mixed short pasta shapes (coloured fussili, penne and farfalle)

Salt to taste

1 tablespoon oil

2 tablespoons butter or oil

2 tablespoons wholewheat flour

2 cups milk + more as required

½ cup grated processed cheese

White pepper powder to taste

½ cup tinned sweetcorn kernels

1 teaspoon finely chopped parsley, to garnish

1 Boil plenty of water in a deep non-stick pan with salt and one tablespoon oil. Add the pasta and cook till *al dente* (cooked but firm to the bite). Drain and set aside.

2 Heat the butter or oil in a non-stick pan. Add the wholewheat flour and sauté lightly, making sure that it does not change colour. Add the milk gradually, stirring continuously, so that no lumps form.

3 Reserve two tablespoons of grated cheese and add the rest to the sauce and continue to stir. After adding the cheese, the sauce will thicken further, so add more milk to adjust the consistency.

4 Add salt and the white pepper powder, and stir. Add the pasta and corn kernels, and mix again.

5 Sprinkle the reserved cheese and chopped parsley on top, and serve.

Chef's Tip:
Add three tablespoons of tomato ketchup and one teaspoon of chilli sauce to the pasta for a spicier dish.

RAINBOW RICE

Sneaking vegetables into rice and pulao is easy! My colleague, Anupa, recommends the use of ketchup, which her younger sister uses liberally to douse the rice. This dish has become a favourite of our younger daughter, Kriti, and her friends too.

2 cups steamed rice

2 tablespoons oil

1 carrot, chopped

1 green capsicum, chopped

¼ cup cabbage, chopped

2 spring onions, chopped

2 teaspoons tomato ketchup

A pinch of black pepper powder

Salt to taste

1 Heat the oil in a non-stick wok; add the carrot, capsicum, cabbage and spring onions, and sauté for four or five minutes.

2 Stir in the rice, tomato ketchup, pepper powder and salt, and mix well. Serve hot.

Chef's Tip:
Add one-fourth cup of hot water just before taking the pan off the heat. It will keep the fried rice nice and moist.

HARI BHARI KHICHDI

Mashed khichdi made with only a dash of ghee and salt is baby food that will keep both toddler and mom happy. Growing kids need more nutritious fare, but that becomes an issue if fussy eating grows side by side! I have added some greens to this khichdi to make a more delicious, attractive and nutritious meal.

¼ cup skinless split green gram

¼ cup shelled green peas

2 stalks spring onion greens, chopped

25 spinach leaves, blanched and puréed

¼ cup rice, soaked

2 tablespoons ghee

½ teaspoon cumin seeds

4 garlic cloves, chopped

5 spring onions, chopped

Salt to taste

1. Pressure-cook the green gram and rice in four cups of water till the pressure is released four times (four whistles).

2. Heat the ghee in a deep non-stick pan. Add the cumin seeds, garlic and spring onions and sauté for two minutes.

3. Add the green peas, spring onion greens and spinach purée, and sauté for a minute.

4. Add the cooked rice and gram mixture and salt, and mix well. Serve hot.

DAL PURI

It is common practice in a Punjabi home to use the previous evening's moong dal to add to the parantha dough to make a quick, nourishing breakfast. The same idea has been used here, except that the dal is freshly made, and I make puri as my kids love them.

½ cup skinless split green gram, soaked

1 cup wholewheat flour

1 teaspoon ginger paste

½ teaspoon coriander powder

¼ teaspoon cumin powder

¼ teaspoon red chilli powder

2 teaspoons chopped fresh coriander

Salt to taste

1 tablespoon oil + for deep-frying

Green Chutney (page 102), as required

1. Boil the split green gram in one and a half cups of water till soft. Set aside to cool.

2. Mix together the boiled gram, wholewheat flour, ginger paste, coriander, cumin and chilli powders, chopped coriander, salt and one tablespoon of oil, and knead into a semi-soft dough.

3. Cover the dough with a damp cloth for about an hour. Divide the dough into marble-sized portions and roll into small balls. Roll out each one into a *puri*.

4. Heat sufficient oil in a non-stick *kadai* and deep-fry the *puri* on medium heat till golden and crisp. Drain on absorbent paper and serve hot with green chutney.

73

POPEYE PULAO

Green rice should intrigue fussy eaters. Garnish with colourful tomatoes or grated carrot. Or better still, just before serving, sprinkle a few shreds of cheese! The play of colours will definitely catch the eye of the fussiest eater.

1 cup rice, soaked and drained

1 medium bunch (250 grams) fresh spinach

1½ tablespoons oil

1 teaspoon cumin seeds

1 medium onion, sliced

6 garlic cloves, crushed

1 green chilli, sliced

Salt to taste

1 Blanch the spinach leaves in hot water for two minutes. Drain and purée in a blender.

2 Heat the oil in a deep non-stick pan and add the cumin seeds. When they begin to change colour, add the onion and garlic, and sauté till translucent. Add the spinach purée and sauté for about five minutes.

3 Stir in the rice, green chilli, salt and two cups of water. Bring to a boil, lower the heat and simmer till the rice is tender. Serve hot.

SECRET NOODLES

This recipe is my colleague Tripta's contribution, as it is her daughter Shreya's favourite dish. The patience to add tempting little touches to a dish is the secret to winning kids' taste buds over. Hence the cheese and peas on toothpicks!

2 packets instant noodles with seasoning

1 medium carrot, cut into small cubes

1 medium tomato, puréed

50 grams processed cheese, cut into ½-inch cubes

¼ cup shelled green peas, blanched

Salt to taste

Toothpicks, as required

1 Heat three cups of water in a non-stick pan; add the noodles, carrot, half the green peas and the seasoning, and bring to a boil.

2 Add the tomato purée and salt if required, and cook until the noodles are tender and the moisture has been absorbed.

3 Thread the cheese cubes and remaining green peas alternately onto toothpicks.

4 Serve the noodles in deep bowls garnished with the cheese-n-pea toothpicks.

PESTO PASTA

Something divine that a pre-teen or teenager would be thrilled to eat!
In fact, this makes a healthy meal for the whole family!

200 grams wholewheat penne
(nib-shaped pasta)

Salt to taste

2 tablespoons olive oil

12-14 baby tomatoes, halved

½ teaspoon crushed red chillies

1 cup milk

2 tablespoons grated Parmesan cheese

Walnut Pesto

8-10 walnut kernels, crushed

¾ cup fresh basil

3-4 garlic cloves

Salt to taste

2 tablespoons olive oil

4 tablespoons grated Parmesan cheese

1 Boil plenty of water in a deep non-stick pan. Add the salt and penne, and cook for fifteen minutes or till *al dente* (cooked but firm to the bite). Drain, mix in one tablespoon of oil and set aside.

2 For the walnut pesto, grind together the walnuts, fresh basil, garlic, salt and olive oil till smooth. Add the Parmesan cheese and grind again.

3 Heat the remaining oil in a non-stick pan and add the baby tomatoes and salt. Cover and cook till the tomatoes soften.

4 Crush the tomatoes with the back of the ladle. Add the walnut pesto and crushed red chillies, and mix well.

5 Stir in the pasta and mix well. Add the milk and cook for another two to three minutes. Sprinkle the Parmesan cheese and serve immediately.

NON-VEGETARIAN MEALS

ANDE KA FUN-DA

Cut the parantha into long strips and have the ketchup on tap!
I remember the ande ke toast my Mom used to make for us when we returned from school.
I have replaced the bread with a flaky parantha and made the meal more substantial.

5 eggs

1 cup wholewheat flour

1 cup refined flour

Salt to taste

1 green chilli, chopped

½ teaspoon carom seeds

2 tablespoons butter

3 tablespoons chopped fresh coriander

5 tablespoons oil

Tomato ketchup, as required

1. Sift together both types of flour with one teaspoon of salt in a bowl. Add the green chilli, carom seeds, one egg and approximately three-fourth cup of water and knead to make a soft dough. Cover with a damp cloth and set aside for one hour.

2. Break four eggs into a separate bowl; add salt and whisk well.

3. Divide the dough into four portions. Roll out each portion into a four-inch round *chapati*. Spread a little butter on each *chapati*, sprinkle a little wholewheat flour and fold it into four.

4. Roll out again on a floured surface into a six-inch square *parantha*.

5. Heat a non-stick *tawa* and place a *parantha* on it. When one side is half cooked, flip it over and spread some beaten egg and chopped coriander on the top. Pour a little oil around the edges and turn over once again.

6. Spread some egg and chopped coriander on the other side as well, and cook till both sides are evenly golden brown.

7. Serve hot with tomato ketchup.

BUTTER CHICKEN

Kriti's friend, Natasha, loves butter chicken. Ever since my sister Namrata showed us this simple recipe,
butter chicken has been in great demand at home, especially when Natasha comes over!

2 tablespoons butter

400 grams skinned, boneless chicken, cut into
1½-inch pieces

1 teaspoon Kashmiri chilli powder

1 tablespoon lemon juice

Salt to taste

A few chopped fresh coriander leaves, to garnish

A few finely cut ginger strips, to garnish

Marinade

½ cup yogurt

2 teaspoons ginger paste

2 teaspoons garlic paste

½ teaspoon Kashmiri chilli powder

½ teaspoon *garam masala* powder

Salt to taste

2 teaspoons mustard oil

Makhni Gravy

2 tablespoons butter

2 green cardamoms

2 cloves

2-3 black peppercorns

1 inch cinnamon

1 teaspoon ginger paste

1 teaspoon garlic paste

½ cup tomato purée

½ teaspoon red chilli powder

Salt to taste

2 tablespoons sugar or honey

½ teaspoon dried fenugreek leaves

½ cup fresh cream

1 Rub a mixture of chilli powder, lemon juice and salt into the chicken and marinate for half an hour in the refrigerator.

2 For the marinade, tie the yogurt in a piece of muslin and hang over a bowl for fifteen to twenty minutes to drain.

3 Transfer the thick yogurt to another bowl. Add the ginger and garlic pastes, chilli and *garam masala* powders, salt and mustard oil.

4 Add the marinade to the chicken and place in the refrigerator for three to four hours to marinate.

5 Preheat an oven to 200°C/400°F/Gas Mark 6.

6 Thread the chicken pieces onto skewers and cook in the preheated oven or a moderately hot *tandoor* for ten to twelve minutes, or until almost done. Baste with butter and cook for another two minutes. Remove and set aside.

7 To make the *makhni* gravy, heat the butter in a non-stick pan. Add the cardamoms, cloves, peppercorns and cinnamon, and sauté for two minutes.

8 Add the ginger and garlic pastes, and sauté for two minutes. Add the tomato purée, chilli powder, salt and half a cup of water, and bring the mixture to a boil. Lower the heat and simmer for ten minutes.

9 Stir in the sugar or honey and powdered dried fenugreek leaves. Add the cooked chicken and cook over low heat for five minutes. Stir in the fresh cream.

10 Garnish with the chopped coriander and ginger strips and serve hot with *naan* or *parantha*.

CHICKEN AND RICE VOLCANO

Build a story around a dish and you will have the kids eating out of your hands! A mound of rice with a steaming curry in the centre will excite the imagination of any child.

Pea Pulao

2 cups steamed rice

½ cup shelled green peas, blanched

1 tablespoon oil

½ teaspoon cumin seeds

Salt to taste

1 tablespoon chopped fresh coriander

Chicken Curry

300 grams skinned, boneless chicken, cut into ½-inch cubes

3 tablespoons oil

3 medium onions, grated

½ tablespoon ginger paste

½ tablespoon garlic paste

¼ teaspoon turmeric powder

1 tablespoon coriander powder

1 teaspoon cumin powder

1 teaspoon red chilli powder

3 medium tomatoes, puréed

Salt to taste

½ teaspoon *garam masala* powder

1 For the pea *pulao*, heat the oil in a non-stick pan and add the cumin seeds. When they change colour, add the green peas, rice and salt. Stir and cook for two minutes.

2 For the chicken curry, heat the oil in a thick-bottomed non-stick pan. Add the onions and sauté till golden brown. Add the ginger and garlic pastes, and continue to sauté for two to three minutes, stirring continuously.

3 Add the turmeric, coriander, cumin and chilli powders, and mix well.

4 Stir in the puréed tomatoes and cook till the oil separates from the *masala*. Add the chicken and salt, and sauté on high heat for five minutes.

5 Add one and a half cups of water, bring to a boil, cover and cook till the chicken is tender. Sprinkle the *garam masala* powder and mix.

6 Heap the rice in the centre of a plate to make a mountain. Press the top down a little and pour some steaming hot curry in the centre.

7 Garnish with the chopped coriander and serve hot.

PEPPY PRAWNS

Children love Chinese food. Crisp fried prawns are a treat for little gourmets. Correction - for gourmets of all sizes! This dish goes perfectly with steamed rice if you make it with a little more gravy.

300 grams king prawns

Salt to taste

½ teaspoon black pepper powder

4 black peppercorns, crushed

2 tablespoons cornflour

2 tablespoons light soy sauce

1½ tablespoons oil + for deep-frying

3 garlic cloves, crushed

¾ inch ginger, chopped

2 spring onions, sliced

3 stalks spring onion greens, sliced

1 Peel the prawns leaving the tails intact; devein and wash thoroughly.

2 In a bowl, combine the salt, one-fourth teaspoon pepper powder, half the crushed peppercorns, one tablespoon of cornflour and one tablespoon of soy sauce. Add the prawns, mix well and set aside to marinate for fifteen minutes. Mix the remaining cornflour with two tablespoons of water.

3 Heat sufficient oil in a non-stick wok and deep-fry the prawns for two minutes. Drain on absorbent paper.

4 In a separate non-stick wok, heat one and a half tablespoons of oil; add the garlic, ginger and spring onions, and sauté for two minutes on high heat.

5 Add the prawns, salt, remaining pepper powder, half the remaining crushed peppercorns, remaining soy sauce, the cornflour mixture and spring onion greens.

6 Stir-fry on high heat for four minutes, or until the prawns are cooked through. Sprinkle the remaining crushed peppercorns and serve hot.

CHICKEN AND CHEESE SPAGHETTI

I know of a few kids who love plain boiled spaghetti! Yes, kids do have tastes that an adult just cannot fathom! But one can add some healthy, fun ingredients like colourful vegetables, chicken and cheese which will make plain old boiled spaghetti really special.

200 grams skinless, boneless chicken breasts, cut into 1-inch pieces

½ cup grated mozzarella cheese

100 grams wholewheat spaghetti

Salt to taste

2 tablespoons oil

4 tablespoons olive oil

6-8 garlic cloves, crushed

¼ cup tomato ketchup

1 small green capsicum, cut into 1-inch pieces

1 small yellow capsicum, cut into 1-inch pieces

½ teaspoon black pepper powder

5-6 fresh basil leaves, roughly torn

1 medium onion, chopped

4-5 fresh button mushrooms, sliced

½ cup blanched and chopped spinach

3 tablespoons cream

1 cup White Sauce (page 102)

1 Cook the spaghetti in boiling salted water till *al dente* (cooked but firm to the bite). Drain, stir in two tablespoons oil and set aside.

2 Heat two tablespoons of olive oil in a non-stick pan. Add half the garlic and sauté till the raw smell disappears.

3 Add the chicken and sauté for five minutes. Add the tomato ketchup and mix. Add the capsicums, salt and one-fourth teaspoon pepper powder. Add the basil leaves and cook till the chicken is tender.

4 Heat two tablespoons of olive oil in another non-stick pan; add the remaining garlic and onion, and sauté for two minutes. Add the button mushrooms and continue to sauté for two to three minutes.

5 Add the spinach, cream, salt and remaining pepper powder, and mix. Remove from heat and set aside.

6 Preheat an oven to 200°C/400°F/Gas Mark 6.

7 Spread half a cup of white sauce at the bottom of a baking dish. Spread half the spaghetti over the sauce and cover with the spinach and mushroom mixture.

8 Sprinkle one-fourth cup of mozzarella cheese and cover with the remaining spaghetti and white sauce.

9 Spread the chicken mixture over the sauce and sprinkle the remaining mozzarella cheese on top. Bake in the preheated oven for fifteen minutes. Serve hot.

SAUCY BUTTERFLIES

My kids love all types of pasta and they are not finicky about it being al dente!
This recipe is perfect for Alyona to make when she is being pestered for something fast,
yummy and nice (read junk food!). But she knows pasta is always a welcome treat (and healthy too).

150 grams farfalle (bow-tie/butterfly) pasta

½ cup minced chicken

1 tablespoon olive oil

1 small onion, chopped

1 garlic clove, crushed

1 carrot, cut into small cubes

2 cups Chicken Stock (page 102)

½ teaspoon dried oregano

Salt to taste

2-3 black peppercorns, crushed

½ cup tomato ketchup

1 small red capsicum, chopped

1 small green capsicum, chopped

1 Heat the oil in a deep non-stick pan. Add the onion, garlic and carrot, and cook for five minutes. Stir in the minced chicken and cook for five minutes longer.

2 Stir in the stock, oregano, salt, crushed peppercorns and tomato ketchup. Add the pasta and the capsicums, and mix well.

3 Cover the pan and cook for ten minutes or till the pasta is *al dente* (cooked but still firm to the bite).

4 The mixture should be, neither too wet nor too dry.

5 Adjust the seasoning and serve hot.

DESSERTS

WAFFLES WITH HONEY AND ICE CREAM

The first time I made this dish was when my niece and nephew, Utsav and Ayushi were spending a summer vacation with us. And guess what happened? None of the children, which included Rachita and Kriti, would stop at just one helping!

1 cup refined flour

1½ teaspoons baking powder

8 tablespoons melted butter

2 tablespoons sugar

A few drops of vanilla essence

2 eggs

¾ cup chilled milk

To Serve

Honey, as required

4 scoops vanilla ice cream

1 Sift the flour and baking powder in a bowl.

2 Cream together six tablespoons of butter and sugar in another bowl. Add the vanilla essence and mix.

3 Break the eggs into the bowl and mix well. Add the flour mixture and mix. Add the milk and whisk to make a smooth batter.

4 Heat a non-stick waffle iron and grease it with a little butter. Pour in a ladleful of batter and lower the lid. Cook till the waffles are golden brown. Gently remove the waffles.

Chef's Tip:
You can also serve the waffles with maple syrup and a dash of lemon juice.

5 Place two waffles on each plate. Drizzle the honey over and top with a scoop of ice cream. Serve immediately.

CHOCO-CUPS

The word cupcake is a term of endearment simply because a cupcake is a dear, sweet little thing!
For birthdays cover with icing and dress them up in cute designs based on a theme. You could write the
guests' names, pipe their initials, draw cute faces, or cover them with coloured vermicelli!

1¾ cups refined flour

60 grams dark cooking chocolate, chopped

100 grams butter + for greasing

1½ cups powdered sugar, sifted

4 eggs, separated

3 teaspoons baking powder

¼ teaspoon salt

½ cup milk

2 teaspoons vanilla essence

Icing

12 tablespoons melted chocolate

8 tablespoons fresh cream

1 tablespoon butter

Multi-coloured chocolate candies, to decorate

1. Preheat an oven to 180°C/350°F/Gas Mark 4. Grease 16 moulds or paper cups.

2. Melt the chocolate in a double boiler or a heat - proof bowl over a pan of simmering water. Add five tablespoons of boiling water to the chocolate and mix well. Cool the mixture slightly.

3. Beat the butter until soft. Add the sugar gradually and beat well until very light and creamy. Beat in one egg yolk at a time. Add the chocolate mixture and mix well.

4. Sift the flour with the baking powder and salt. Mix together the milk and vanilla essence. Add the flour mixture in three parts to the butter-sugar mixture alternately with the milk. Beat the batter until smooth after each addition.

5. Whip the egg whites until stiff but not dry. Fold them lightly into the cake batter.

6. Pour the batter into the prepared moulds or paper cups till two-third full and bake in the preheated oven for thirty minutes. Remove from the oven and place on a wire rack to cool.

7. For the icing, mix together the melted chocolate with the fresh cream and butter till well blended.

8. Spread the icing over the cooled cupcakes. Sprinkle a few chocolate candies on top of each cupcake and serve.

FIGALICIOUS PUDDING

I love baking this pudding during winter, as it fills me with a warm, happy feeling. Dates and figs make a healthy combination. Dates are a high-carbohydrate food, rich in fiber and packed with sugar, while figs are packed with essential nutrients. So make this pudding, but don't reveal the ingredients to your kids. It's good for them, it's good for us, so let's dig in!

14 seedless dates, chopped

4-5 dried figs, chopped

1 fresh fig, quartered, to garnish (optional)

½ teaspoon sodium bicarbonate

85 grams refined flour

1 teaspoon baking powder

½ cup walnuts, chopped

200 grams sweetened condensed milk

½ cup butter

½ teaspoon vanilla essence

8-10 almonds, slivered

½ cup milk

Custard Sauce

2½ tablespoons custard powder

2½ cups milk

4 tablespoons brown sugar

1 Preheat an oven to 150°C/300°F/Gas Mark 2.

2 Cook the dates and figs in one-fourth cup of water with the sodium bicarbonate, stirring continuously. Set aside to cool.

3 Sift the flour with the baking powder into a bowl. Add the date and fig mixture along with the walnuts and mix well.

4 Place the condensed milk and butter in a bowl and whisk well to mix. Add the flour mixture and vanilla essence, and mix well.

5 Transfer the mixture to two greased oven-proof ramekins (small moulds) and spread evenly. Sprinkle the almond slivers and bake in the preheated oven for about fifty minutes. The puddings are done if a thin knife or skewer inserted into them comes out clean.

6 Remove the puddings from the oven and set aside to cool for ten minutes. Heat the milk and pour over the puddings.

7 For the custard sauce, mix the custard powder with half a cup of milk. Heat the remaining milk in a non-stick pan. Add the brown sugar and stir till it dissolves.

8 When the mixture comes to a boil, add the custard powder mixture and cook, stirring continuously, till the mixture thickens and coats the back of the spoon.

9 Unmould the puddings onto plates, pour the sauce over and decorate with the fresh figs. Serve warm.

SWEET APPLE SURPRISE

One of the easiest and tastiest desserts ever - children are going to lap this one up!
Give the dish a little twist by adding oats to give it an interesting texture and make it
more nutritious. My older daughter Rachita likes a sprinkling of crushed peanut chikki on top.

5 medium apples

200 grams sweetened condensed milk

6 tablespoons butter

½ teaspoon cinnamon powder

¾ cup refined flour

1 Preheat an oven to 180°C/350°F/Gas Mark 4.

2 Mix together the condensed milk and one and a half tablespoons of butter in a non-stick pan and heat the mixture gently for two to three minutes. Remove from heat and set aside to cool. Stir in half the cinnamon powder.

3 Peel and slice the apples. Arrange the apple slices in layers in a six-inch round oven-proof dish, pressing down lightly. Pour the condensed milk mixture over the apples and spread it evenly.

4 In a bowl, mix together the refined flour, remaining butter and remaining cinnamon powder with your fingertips till the mixture resembles breadcrumbs. Sprinkle generously over the apples, so as to cover them completely.

5 Bake in the preheated oven for forty-five minutes, or till the crumble topping turns golden brown. Serve hot or warm.

MANGO MAZAA

When they say haste makes waste they did not know about this fantastic recipe!
Simply measure, mix, and freeze! This nutritious ice cream for your family can be made
with your kid's favourite fruit. Use ice lolly, kulfi or other fancy moulds to make the ice cream more tempting.

1 cup cream

1 cup mango pulp

1 cup milk powder

1 cup sugar

1 cup chilled milk

1 Blend all the ingredients in a blender till smooth. Pour into a glass bowl and cover tightly, or fill in moulds and place in a freezer to set.

2 Scoop out into bowls or unmould and serve immediately.

Chef's Tip:
If the mango pulp is very sweet, reduce the amount of sugar.

MANGO KIWI DUET

It was one of my proudest moments when our older daughter Rachita cooked this recipe at an inter-school cookery competition and won the 1st prize. What makes this dessert more memorable is that she concocted this recipe all by herself.

2 medium ripe mangoes, chopped

1 kiwi fruit, sliced

4 cups *kesari shrikhand*

20 sweet biscuits such as glucose biscuits

20 chocolate cream wafer biscuits

4 tablespoons butter, melted

Glazed cherries, to decorate

1 Grease the base of an eight-inch springform cake tin with a little melted butter. Crush the sweet biscuits in a blender. Transfer to a bowl, add the melted butter and mix.

2 Spread the mixture on the greased base of the cake tin and press down lightly. Arrange the chocolate wafer biscuits along the sides of the cake tin.

3 Add the mangoes to the *shrikhand* and mix well. Pour the mango *shrikhand* over the biscuit layer and arrange the kiwi slices around the outer edge.

4 Arrange the cherries in the middle and chill till set. Remove the pudding from the tin and serve.

CHOCO-CHIP PUDDING

This is a classic, English bread and butter pudding, which is a favourite in my home. Adding chocolate chips, always a favourite with children, is going to make it more appealing. You could replace the chocolate chips with crushed praline or chikki.

½ cup chocolate chips

8 slices brown bread

3 tablespoons butter

2 cups hot milk

½ cup brown sugar

2 tablespoons cocoa powder

4 eggs, whisked

A few drops of vanilla essence

1 Preheat an oven to 180°C/350°F/Gas Mark 4.

2 Spread the butter on the bread slices. Place one slice on top of the other and make four sandwiches. Cut each sandwich into four triangles. Arrange the triangles in a six-inch square baking dish so that one triangle overlaps another.

3 Pour the hot milk in a bowl, add the sugar and stir till it dissolves. Add the cocoa powder and mix well. Add the eggs and whisk to mix well. Add the vanilla essence and mix again.

4 Pour the mixture over the bread and press it down lightly so that the bread soaks up most of the milk. Sprinkle the chocolate chips on top. Place the dish in the preheated oven and bake for about forty minutes. Serve hot or cold.

GOLDEN CASTLES

Small servings of pudding go down well with kids. The caramel colour reminds me of small sand castles we build with kids on the beach, only this one has a glistening gold topping. You can decorate or surround it with fresh fruit or colourful chocolate or candy buttons.

6 tablespoons sugar

¾ cup thick yogurt

¾ tin (300 grams) condensed milk

¾ cup milk

15 raisins

10 almonds, blanched, peeled and slivered

1 Place the sugar in a thick-bottomed non-stick pan. Add a few drops of water and heat till the sugar caramelises. Pour the caramel into four small moulds and leave to set.

2 Heat sufficient water in a pressure cooker. Place the condensed milk in a deep bowl. Add the milk and yogurt and whisk together till well blended. Pour the mixture into four heat-proof moulds. Sprinkle the raisins on the top.

3 Cover the moulds with cling film to seal well. Make a few slits in the cling film and place the moulds in the pressure cooker. Cover the cooker and steam, without the weight, for about forty minutes.

4 Take the moulds out of the pressure cooker and set aside to cool to room temperature. Chill in a refrigerator.

5 Just before serving, turn the moulds upside down to unmould the desserts, so that the liquid gold caramel is on top. Garnish with almond slivers and serve.

STRAWBERRY SWIRLIES

Why buy ready-made fruit yogurt when you can easily whip up some at home? Be creative and top it with a sprinkling of chocolate shavings.

10-12 strawberries, chopped

2 cups thick yogurt, whisked

2 tablespoons powdered sugar

2 scoops vanilla ice cream

1 Tie up the yogurt in a piece of muslin and hang over a bowl, preferably in a refrigerator, to drain.

2 Mix together the drained yogurt, sugar and ice cream. Reserve two tablespoons of the chopped strawberries and add the rest to the yogurt mixture and process in a blender.

3 Spoon into four bowls and place in a refrigerator to chill. Sprinkle the reserved strawberries on top and serve.

ANNEXURE

CHICKEN STOCK

Boil 200 grams chicken bones in water for 5 minutes. Drain and discard water. Boil blanched bones with a roughly chopped carrot, celery stalk, leek, 2-3 parsley stalks, 6-7 black peppercorns, 5-6 cloves, 1 bay leaf and 10 cups of water. Remove any scum which rises to the surface and replace it with more cold water. Simmer for at least 1 hour. Remove from heat, strain, cool and store in a refrigerator till further use.

DATE AND TAMARIND CHUTNEY

Wash, stone and chop 15-20 dates. Dry-roast 2 teaspoons cumin seeds and ¼ teaspoon fennel seeds. Cool and grind to a powder. Cook the dates, 1 cup tamarind pulp, cumin and fennel powder, ½ cup jaggery, 2 teaspoons red chilli powder, 1 teaspoon dried ginger powder, black salt, salt and four cups of water till thick.

EGGLESS MAYONNAISE

Whisk together ¼ cup cream, ¼ teaspoon mustard paste, ½ teaspoon lemon juice, ½ teaspoon black pepper powder and salt to taste in a clean dry bowl. Add ¾ cup oil a little by little, whisking continuously, till all the oil is incorporated.

GREEN CHUTNEY

Grind together 1 cup fresh coriander, ½ cup fresh mint, 2-3 green chillies, black salt to taste, ¼ teaspoon sugar and 1 tablespoon lemon juice to a smooth paste using a little water if required.

SALSA

Roast 2 halved large onions, 5 halved garlic cloves, 4 halved medium tomatoes and 1 quartered capsicum on a hot griddle till the skins are charred. Cool and grind coarsely with salt. Transfer to a bowl and stir in the lemon juice.

VEGETABLE STOCK

Peel, wash and chop 1 onion, ½ medium carrot, 2-3 inch celery stalk and 2-3 garlic cloves. Place in a pan with 1 bay leaf, 5-6 peppercorns, 2-3 cloves and 5 cups of water and bring to a boil. Lower heat and simmer for 15 minutes and strain. Cool and store in a refrigerator till further use.

WHITE SAUCE

Melt 2 tablespoons butter in a heavy-bottomed pan and stir in 2 tablespoons refined flour. Cook for five to six minutes over low heat till fragrant. Whisk in 2 cups milk till smooth. Cook for four to five minutes, stirring continuously, till the sauce thickens. Add salt to taste and ½ teaspoon white pepper powder and mix well. Strain the sauce. Makes 2 cups.

GLOSSARY

English	Hindi
Basil	Tulsi
Bean sprouts	Ankurit moong
Beaten rice	Poha
Button mushrooms	Khumb
Cardamoms, green	Chhoti elaichi
Carom seeds	Ajwain
Cinnamon	Dalchini
Cottage cheese	Paneer
Cream, fresh	Malai
Cumin seeds	Jeera
Dates	Khajur
Dried figs	Anjeer
Fennel seeds	Saunf
Finger millet	Ragi
Gram flour	Besan
Gram, green skinless split	Dhuli moong dal
Gram, black skinless split	Dhuli urad dal
Gram, whole green	Sabut moong
Honey	Shahad
Maize flour	Makai ka atta
Musk melon	Kharbooj
Mustard seeds	Rai/sarson
Parboiled rice	Ukda chawal
Parsley	Ajmoda
Pomegranate seeds, dried	Anardana
Raisins	Kishmish
Refined flour	Maida
Semolina	Rawa/sooji
Shallots	Chhote pyaaz
Sweetcorn kernels	Makai ke dane
Vinegar	Sirka
Walnuts	Akhrot
Wholewheat flour	Atta

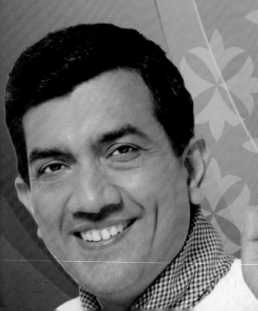